Wants versus Needs

Clothes

Linda Staniford

raintree

a Capstone company — publishers for children

Raintree is an imprint of Capstone Global Library Limited, a company incorporated in England and Wales having its registered office at 7 Pilgrim Street, London, EC4V 6LB – Registered company number: 6695582

www.raintreepublishers.co.uk
myorders@raintreepublishers.co.uk

Edited by Linda Staniford and Shelly Lyons
Designed by Philippa Jenkins
Original illustrations © Capstone Global Library Ltd 2015
Picture research by Tracy Cummins
Production by Helen McCreath
Originated by Capstone Global Library Ltd
Printed and bound in China

ISBN 978 1 406 29060 8
18 17 16 15 14
10 9 8 7 6 5 4 3 2 1

British Library Cataloguing in Publication Data
A full catalogue record for this book is available from the British Library.

Acknowledgements
We would like to thank the following for permission to reproduce photographs: Alamy: imageBROKER, 19; Capstone Press: Philippa Jenkins, Cover Top, design elements; Getty Images: J. Parsons, 20, 23, Jack Hollingsworth, 4, Mieke Dalle, 16, Rob Lewine, 18, 22 BR; Shutterstock: Alena Ozerova, 6, 22 TL, Back Cover, Christina Richards, 21, Goodluz, 12, 23, HandmadePictures, 23, Kzenon, 5, MaszaS, 7, Monkey Business Images, 10, 13, 23 oliveromg, 11, Pressmaster, 23, siamionau pavel, 1, Cover Bottom, spotmatik, 15; Thinkstock: Barry Austin Photography, 14, 22 BR, Seiya Kawamoto, 17, SerrNovik, 8, 22 TR, Stockbyte, 9

Every effort has been made to contact copyright holders of material reproduced in this book. Any omissions will be rectified in subsequent printings if notice is given to the publisher.

Disclaimer
All the internet addresses (URLs) given in this book were valid at the time of going to press. However, due to the dynamic nature of the internet, some addresses may have changed, or sites may have changed or ceased to exist since publication. While the author and publisher regret any inconvenience this may cause readers, no responsibility for any such changes can be accepted by either the author or the publisher.

Contents

Some words are shown in bold, **like this**. You can find them in the glossary on page 23.

What are needs and wants?

Needs are things that help us to live. We need some clothes to **protect** us. Some clothes we want because we like them. We do not need them.

You need clothes to keep you warm
in winter, and to protect your skin from
the sun in summer.

What do we need to wear in winter?

In winter, you need to wear thick clothes to keep you warm outdoors.

You need to wear more than shorts and
T-shirts during winter. You need a thick
coat, boots, a hat and gloves.

What do we need to wear in summer?

In summer, you need to wear things that will **protect** you from the sun. Sunglasses protect your eyes from the bright sunlight.

8

You do not need a woolly hat in the summer. You need a sunhat to protect your head and face from the sun's rays.

Smart or casual clothes?

It is important to wear the right clothes at the right times.

You may want to wear jeans and a T-shirt. But for a special event like a wedding, you need to wear **smart** clothes.

What kind of shoes do we need to wear?

It is important to wear the right kind of shoes for what you are doing. When you are walking around a lot, you need strong, **comfortable** shoes.

You may want to wear your comfortable shoes all the time. But there are some times when you need to wear **smart** shoes.

What do we need to wear to play sports?

If you play sport for a team, you want to wear the team's colours. It is also important to wear the right clothes for the sport you play.

Some people need to wear clothing that **protects** them. Cyclists need to wear cycle helmets.

Do we need new and old clothes?

Sometimes our clothes get too small or begin to wear out. When this happens we need new clothes. But do you need lots of clothes?

Keeping old clothes is useful. You can wear them if you are doing something messy. This means your newer clothes will stay clean.

Do we need to wear pretty things or useful things?

Some things you wear you may not need. Jewellery looks nice with a party dress or **smart** outfit. But do you need jewellery?

Lots of people like to wear a watch. Watches are useful because they tell us the time. We need a watch if we have to be somewhere at a certain time.

Do we need designer clothes?

Some of your friends might wear **designer clothes**. You may want to wear designer clothes too. But they cost a lot of money. You do not need them.

You do not always need new clothes.
Second-hand shops offer many great
bargains.

Quiz

Are these clothes needs or wants?

Picture glossary

 **comfortable** feeling at ease

 **designer clothes** clothes that are made by a famous designer

 **expensive** costing a lot of money

 **protect** keep safe from danger

 **smart** neat and tidy

Index

Note to parents and teachers

Reading non-fiction texts for information is an important part of a child's literary development. Readers can be encouraged to ask simple questions and then use the text to find the answers. Each chapter in this book begins with a question. Read the questions together. Look at the pictures. Talk about what the answer might be. Then read the text to find out if your predictions were correct. To develop readers' enquiry skills, encourage them to think of other questions they might ask about the topic. Discuss where you could find the answers. Assist children in using the contents page, picture glossary and index to practise research skills and new vocabulary.